COUNTRY FARMHOUSE

COUNTRY FARMHOUSE

CINDY SMITH COOPER

83 PRESS

Hoffman Media
1900 International Park Drive, Suite 50
Birmingham, Alabama 35243
hoffmanmedia.com

83
PRESS

ISBN # 978-1-940772-62-2
Printed in China

TABLE OF CONTENTS

INTRODUCTION

There is something profoundly sentimental and blissfully idyllic about the classic country farmhouse. Undoubtedly one of the most popular styles in North America today, this iconic look speaks to our hearts and souls with a deep reverence for family and history, warmth and comfort, hearth and home. No matter its location—set amidst a sprawling bucolic landscape of ponds, fields, and trees, or tucked within a thriving city suburb—the country farmhouse is a quintessential rural scene that radiates with individual expression and an unmistakable sense of Old-World style.

As prevalent in Cape Cod as it is on the West Coast, the country farmhouse continues to shape our decorating tastes even today. Forever an alluring source of inspiration, the country farmhouse provides a rich heritage of architecture and design—from simple clapboard country homes and charming red barns to timeworn heirloom antiques and flea market treasures uncovered while engaging in the thrill of the hunt. The delightful notion that the classic country farmhouse first and foremost captures the individual tastes of the dwellers within may very well be the reason for its broad universal appeal. Each home—whether a modest seaside saltbox or a refined plantation home passed down for generations—offers a pleasing and often whimsical mix of meaningful finds and collectibles that truly reflect the personalities and lifestyles of the homeowners.

For many of us, the classic farmhouse lives only in our imaginations or in fleeting images glimpsed from the roadside while journeying through the country. To others, it is a self-sustaining way of life, a symbol of family pride, and a tribute to our agricultural heritage. But whatever image lives in your mind's eye, the authentic farmhouses still standing are treasured survivors of our North American history, relics from a bygone era that are today being reclaimed and restored in a number of creative ways from coast to coast.

Across the country, newly constructed homes are also following suit, replicating the hand-hewn charm and rustic romance of the North American vernacular farmhouse. Adorned with timeworn architectural details—reclaimed wood floors, ceiling beams gouged and imperfect, recycled brick and stone—these dwellings, whether ancient or modern, exude a distinctive sincerity and homey warmth like no other. Today, farmhouse style can exist in the suburbs just as easily as it can at an

inviting lakeside retreat or amidst a sprawling rural acreage, where other pursuits are often enjoyed—horse farming, gardening, lavish barn dinners, guest- and pool-house entertaining—and where families have plenty of space to spread out and relax.

Filled to the brim with cherished antique accents such as vintage quilts and textiles, wood-burning stoves, beautifully distressed furniture pieces, and flea-market collectibles, today's country farmhouse represents home for all walks of life, from solitude-seeking artists and writers, to multigenerational families and organic farmers.

The simple elegance of country farmhouse style stems from an enchanting combination of comfort and timeless beauty. Ranging from the vintage to the industrial—and adorned with charming features such as rustic siding, subdued paint hues, and a multitude of windows that flood the interior spaces with captivating natural sunlight—the homes pictured on these pages sing with exquisite personal taste and a liberating sense of individuality. Whether a new pastoral build that honors the past or a weathered weekend getaway, the farmhouse-style dwellings that fill this extraordinary collection epitomize the true spirit of hearth and home.

Colonial Charm

A SNOWBALLING RENOVATION TRANSFORMED THIS ONCE-QUAINT STRUCTURE INTO A SPRAWLING COUNTRY HOME FILLED WITH FRESH COLORS, STORIED ANTIQUES, AND PLENTY OF ROOM FOR GATHERING— ALL WHILE STAYING TRUE TO THE ORIGINAL SPIRIT OF THE HOME.

uilt in the 1830s, the farmhouse nestled among the rolling green hills of New York started life simply. From sheep herders to the owners of a silver company, the home passed from family to family, gathering history until, two decades ago, a new chapter began. "We bought it in 1998, when it was just the little house," says the homeowner. "Not much work had been done to it."

With the help of architect Jimmy Crisp and builder George Carrothers, the new homeowners set about executing the necessary updates. They started small—raising door frames and opening ceilings to expose original beams—but it wasn't long before they added a porch and replaced the roof with one featuring dormers. "The renovation just continued snowballing," the homeowner adds.

Eventually, the string of projects led to a full addition designed to give the family everything they needed while enhancing—but not obscuring—the original structure's Colonial charm. "We took our cues from the original house and mixed it with some period detailing," says Jimmy. He adds that the final design "felt comfortable to the vernacular architecture of the region and the time" while respecting the original farmhouse.

Because the original structure was built south-facing with a driveway on the north, the family mainly used the kitchen door to enter the home. For the new house, they found inspiration in a side hall-style home in Massachusetts. "We designed it to have an entry that went from the front to the back of the house, where you could look out at the beautiful fields out back," the homeowner says.

A winding stone wall paints a line of rustic beauty through the countryside outside of the farmhouse. Rippling with hills, the property was the perfect place for the former owners to raise sheep.

Along with adding four bedrooms to the existing three, the new structure provided a fresh living room with high ceilings and plenty of windows. It's an airy space that's reflective of the spirit of the rest of the home, which is saturated with bright neutrals and cheery tones anchored by antique character.

"I studied art history in school," says the homeowner, "and history has always fascinated me." That interest, along with time spent in France with her husband, sparked a love for the antique pieces that now fill the home. "Bringing back a lot of the French antiques was a way of bringing some of that culture and history back to our home," she says. "We tried to pair them and have them flow with the other older and more American-style antiques."

Because they didn't want the old house to fall into disuse, the homeowners opted to continue using the original dining room—once a weaving room—for formal entertaining. To create the more casual dining space they needed, they placed a long table by the bank of windows in the kitchen. "We really wanted to have a room that was light and bright where you could look out and see the fields," the homeowner says, "and that is really the area where we spend most of our time playing games or dining or just sitting around having coffee."

Enjoying the view was a priority in the master bedroom as well, where a custom shade of green creates a serene aura and draws in the beauty outside. "We felt that the green was an appropriate way to bring the verdant forests and fields around us into the home," the homeowner says, "because we would come from the city to the country and wanted to be surrounded by that nature."

As in the rest of the home, classic lines and sunny tones are balanced by darker shades and attention to detail. From the floor plan to the furnishings, each element of the design merges to create a cohesive design that breathes new life into a long-cherished home.

In contrast to the sunny style of the rest of the home, the library features a deep navy tone on the walls. Bright white shelves lighten the room, and a painting that the homeowners received as a gift upon their son's birth adorns one wall.

"Since we lived in the city and this was a place for the weekends, we wanted to have more guests and family come out," says the homeowner. "So, we wanted the addition to have enough bedrooms." Along with four additional sleeping spaces, the farmhouse, which is 25 minutes from the closest store, also has a large pantry and double fridge, perfect for stocking up.

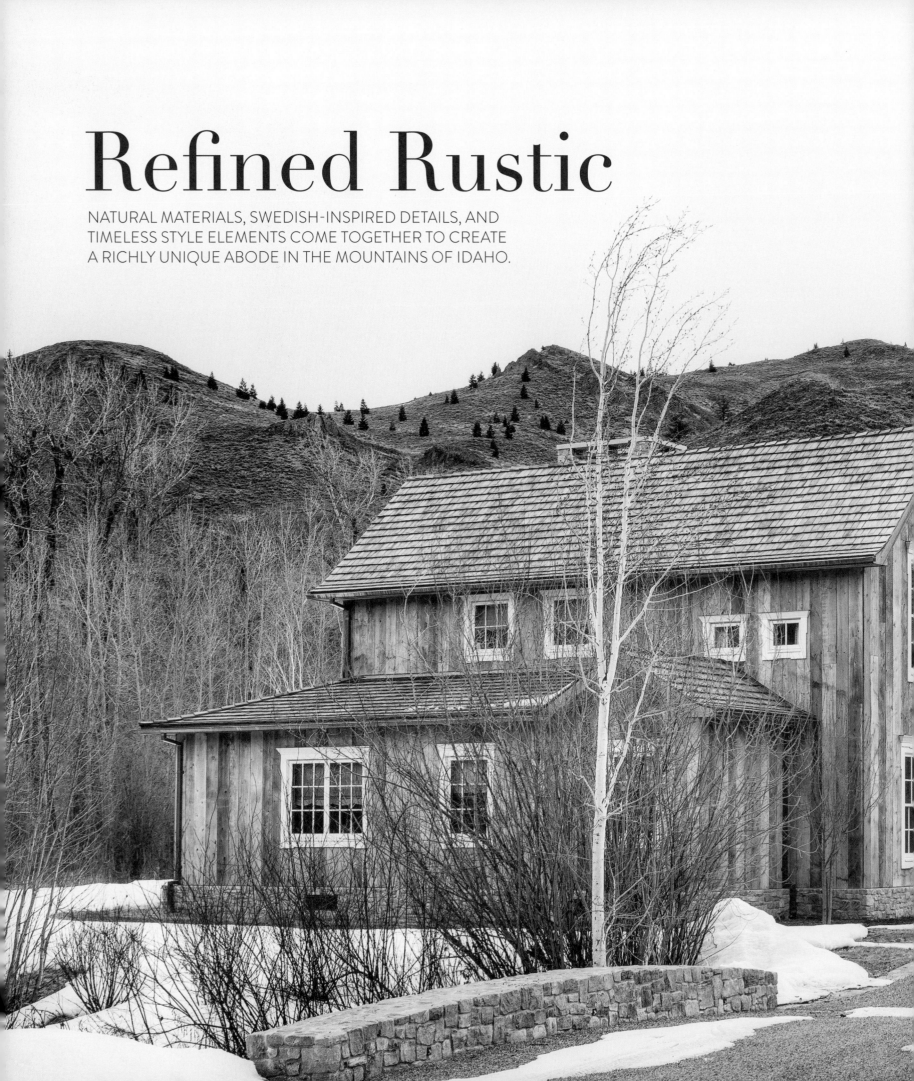

Refined Rustic

NATURAL MATERIALS, SWEDISH-INSPIRED DETAILS, AND
TIMELESS STYLE ELEMENTS COME TOGETHER TO CREATE
A RICHLY UNIQUE ABODE IN THE MOUNTAINS OF IDAHO.

At first glance, the riverside mountain home has all the traits of a classic farmhouse. Surrounded by breathtaking views, the custom-built structure is dotted with dormers and features vertical planked siding in rich, varied shades of barn wood. "Because of all the aspen and cottonwoods on the site, we wanted to keep the color tone in the aspen trunk color," says architect Janet Jarvis of The Jarvis Group. She worked alongside the homeowners to create a space that breathes traditional farmhouse style—but with a twist.

"They wanted to do something that felt farmhouse-like and that fit the area, but they just liked the aesthetics of Swedish design," Janet says. "So, we moved in that direction." She points out details like the white windows and trim that contrast against the darker wood siding, as well as the subtle swoop of the roof. Reminiscent of classic Swedish design elements, they complement the rustic mountain charm of the home's exterior.

Inside, the design leans heavily into clean and classic style. Tumbled Montana moss rock and reclaimed barn timbers ground quaint, traditional furniture, and a color palette of serene blues and creams softens the more rustic elements. In an effort to make the house feel timeless, the designers selected hand-hewn, wire-brushed oak flooring from Europe. "We stayed more traditional than contemporary, and we tried to stay very true to the Swedish style," Janet says.

In the kitchen, the warm gray tones of the planked ceiling and oak floors frame custom-designed cabinets painted in a robin's egg blue.

One of the home's four fireplaces provides added warmth to an already cozy gathering space. Floral drapes soften the mountain lodge atmosphere, heightening the room's relaxing properties, and a vaulted ceiling keeps the plush furniture from feeling too crowded.

"We spent a great deal of time on the cabinet design," says Janet, noting that the layout was meant to preserve and enhance the river view outside the window. Diamond details on the upper cabinet doors are part of a motif seen throughout the entire home, and a raised fireplace is visible from both the island and the adjacent dining space, injecting extra warmth into family dinners.

The farm table in the dining area features a dark finish, contrasting with the weathered beige paint of the ladder-back chairs, and sky blue gingham cushions contribute a touch of color and comfort. At one end of the space, a built-in hutch houses the family's glassware. "It's very traditional and Swedish to soften all the cabinets," Janet says of the fabric panels that cover the glass doors at each end of the hutch.

When it comes to relaxation, the family has plenty of areas to choose from. "We always try to complement the exterior dormer style, and they become such great places to hang out and read," Janet says of the many nooks and window seats throughout the home. Furnished with plush cushions and throw pillows, the spaces are perfect for spending time alone reading, doing homework, or just enjoying the view. But when it comes time for gathering with friends and family, the downstairs game room offers a billiard table and plenty of places to sit back and enjoy the laughter.

At the end of the day, the homeowners unwind in a master bedroom made light with pale tones and classic patterns. "The fabrics are fairly delicate," Janet says, noting the care that went into selecting the textiles. A pair of cozy cream chairs by the fire offers a spot to curl up, reflect on the day's events, and watch the snow fall from the comfort of the fireside. It's a thoroughly classic space touched with rustic warmth from the rough-hewn ceiling beams and plaster walls.

The blend of styles is evident in every inch of the home, inside and out, resulting in a design that feels fresh yet ageless. "I would say it's a very refined rustic," says Janet, pointing out the home's subtle updated edge. She notes her philosophy of combining old elements with new products—a technique that, in this case, resulted in the perfect marriage of classic farmhouse charm and Scandinavian style.

With a subdued color palette and patterns leaning toward the understated, the design relies on various textures for warmth and interest. Plaster walls, unpainted wood, and details such as wool fabric on the walls of the game room add a sense of history and character to the home's interior.

A charming desk is the perfect place to jot a quick note by the sunlight from the windows. In the master bathroom, calming hues are paired with the warmth of the oak flooring for a truly serene space.

Although the planked vaulted ceiling offers a sense of openness, this guest bedroom remains cozy due to the warm neutrals and layered patterns on the bed. The creamy tones are balanced by darker touches in the window hardware and chandelier.

The careful selection of textiles is evident in one of the home's three guest rooms, where textures and patterns are balanced perfectly with neutral tones. A cozy chair in one corner provides a hint of blush.

A Personal Touch

FACED WITH AN OPPORTUNITY TO CREATE A SPACE SUITED TO THEIR PERSONAL
STYLES, THESE HOMEOWNERS DOVE RIGHT INTO THE PROJECT AND CRAFTED
A LABOR OF LOVE OVERFLOWING WITH ENCHANTING FRENCH STYLE.

One of the home's bolder color choices, the sliding barn door that opens to the laundry room features a distressed shade of mint. A sleek bench with a touch of French elegance waits against the wall of the hallway outside.

The home was purchased with the intent to renovate. With a charming location on a quiet lane, it was the perfect place for the homeowners' needs, but there were more than a few problems with the interior. "It was a complete remodel," says interior designer Amy Studebaker of Amy Studebaker Design. "Most of the interior of the home was taken down to the framework and then redesigned."

A layout that was portioned into small, intimate spaces wasn't conducive to the homeowners' lifestyle, and an interior design style that leaned toward the formal didn't match their personalities. With the help of Amy, designer Michelle Thore and architect David Pape of Pape Studio Architects planned a new layout that would transform the home into an open-concept space designed to strike a balance between formal and casual—something that was important to the homeowners.

The end result is a farmhouse glowing with serene, neutral tones and subtle texture chosen to enrich but not dominate the design. "The subdued palette, along with the mixing of antique and new pieces, created an environment that's fresh and refined, as well as warm and effortless," says one of the homeowners.

According to Amy, white oak wood flooring with a soft gray finish and antiqued pavers were used throughout the home to create a backdrop perfect for layering furniture, rugs, and accessories. For added texture, the walls and ceiling were treated with white plaster. "A subtle technique was requested for the plaster application to allow for an elegant ambiance," Amy says.

That ambiance fills the hearth room, where the homeowners like to gather with family. The plaster finish is paired with reclaimed ceiling beams and classic furniture featuring muted shades of red and blue. Deep, cozy club chairs and an inviting sofa are well-suited to relaxation—the perfect touch to a soft, calming space ideal for hosting intimate get-togethers.

The room was designed to flow naturally into the kitchen, where warm gray tones deepen the creamy hues of the design. "Minimal upper cabinets were hung, and the refrigerator columns were separated with floating shelves placed between to create a wall that felt as though it was holding a furniture piece," Amy says. Backing the shelves and range, glossy gray subway tile adds a touch of interest to the space, and a hood over the range was plastered and faux finished to create an aged texture.

When it came to renovating the master bedroom, there were plenty of changes that needed to be made in order to create the serene refuge that the homeowners needed. "The master bedroom consisted of multiple closets spread throughout the suite, a bathroom which opened off of a hallway, and a master sitting room which proportionately felt wrong for the direction we wanted to take the space," Amy says.

To correct the issues, the architect consolidated the closets into a single dressing room and made the bathroom accessible from the bedroom. The painted planked ceiling, from which hangs an elegant chandelier, creates an open atmosphere made airy by the creamy tones and abundant sunlight in the space. The room is anchored by an upholstered gray bed that, along with the nightstands and armoire, speak of a subtle, romantic French influence inspired by the original architectural style of the home's exterior.

The architect also lowered the ceiling of the master sitting room, creating a more comfortable personal corner of the home that flows more naturally with the layout. Subdued patterns layer the space, and a fireplace adorned with detailed carvings is flanked by a set of enclosed shelves featuring a weathered finish.

Although the challenge that the home originally presented might have sent another couple searching for an easier option, these homeowners were able to see past the surface to the potential beneath. In the end, the decision to treat the home with a little tough love created an open, relaxing farmhouse filled with understated elegance, effortless grace, and plenty of room to enjoy the company of loved ones.

The ceiling in the dining room is planked with wood featuring a natural, gray finish, heightening the space's warmth and adding an atmosphere of intimacy. A graceful chandelier contributes a feminine touch, and the windows in one wall provide a vibrant view of the outdoors.

The master bathroom is surrounded with gray shiplap that adds a touch of texture and contrasts with the lighter tile of the floor. A hint of warmth was introduced in the form of a weathered rug, and the simple yet sophisticated drawer pulls are the perfect finishing detail.

In contrast to the bright, creamy hues used throughout the rest of the home, the study is painted a darker, moody tone, providing a level of masculine style.

Cultivating Home

A SOUTH CAROLINA FAMILY
RELOCATES TO THEIR
VACATION FARMHOUSE
AND EMBARKS ON A
DESIGN PROCESS TO GIVE
THE ABODE A SENSE OF
UTMOST AUTHENTICITY.

After a decade of enjoying their vacation home on 140 acres of verdant working farmland in South Carolina, Leslie and Bob Harris decided to make a permanent move to their peaceful haven—but not without substantial fine-tuning to suit Leslie's clear, creative vision.

It all started in 2000, after they stumbled upon the house for sale while visiting Bob's hometown of Indian Land. They purchased it on the spot, bringing the property that had belonged to his great-grandfather—and subsequent generations—back into the family. Situated on a road named for Bob's grandfather, the farm had been sold in the '90s to another family who replaced the existing home with a quaint farmhouse.

For 10 years, the property served as a weekend getaway for Bob, Leslie, and their six children. When the couple made it their primary residence, Leslie decided to play up its idyllic appeal and craft a charming cottage with French Country style. "We knew we'd be here for the rest of our lives, so we started a major renovation," she says.

A wraparound porch was added to meet a large screened veranda, offering ample views of scenic pastures and ponds. To create better flow and promote fellowship, the Harrises removed walls to open the living room to the kitchen and a small porch that they converted into a sunroom.

A nurse by profession, Leslie has always been a decorating enthusiast, so she was excited to try a new aesthetic in their pastoral setting. Knowing she wanted to infuse the abode with a rustic ambience, she sold the furnishings that filled their previous traditional-style home. All they brought with them

Homeowners Leslie and Bob Harris created an inviting open floor plan by removing a wall between the living room and renovating the kitchen. The outcome is a charming whitewashed space brimming with bucolic touches like open shelving, which showcases both distressed wooden accessories and polished wares. Notes of green, from accents like the pendant lights to arrangements of natural bounty, echo the lush farmland surrounds.

was their piano. "This farm had been in Bob's family for a long time, and I wanted everything to look like it belonged," Leslie explains.

The new pieces come from near and far, acquired through traveling and antiquing—hobbies the couple enjoys. "Most of what is in this house are things we have collected on travels," Leslie says. "Rarely do I look for something for a specific area of the house. If I love it, I buy it, and I know I'm going to find somewhere for it."

Many accents, from decorative linens to an extensive blue-and-white porcelain collection, came from a buying tour in France, while the aged wood elements incorporated throughout have been salvaged from barns and old structures across town. One of the barns even belonged to Bob's grandfather and yielded the bark wood to build the master bed.

Countless other fixtures are passed-down or repurposed heirlooms, found around the farm or in the area. With these treasured finds, Bob, who holds a Ph.D. in wood science, constructs many things Leslie commissions, including tables, bookshelves, benches, headboards, and more. "There's very little we have found on the property or in this community that we don't keep," Leslie says.

Throughout the decorating journey, Leslie has grown attached to the color white, and the serene hue creates a calming palette across the home. "White looks clean. It's simple and timeless," she says. While she loves to paint their abundance of reclaimed wood in her favorite shade, Bob sometimes draws the line with wood he deems too precious, like the sawed mahogany hand-carved bed in a guest room.

Leslie's ultimate goal was to instill the feel of home in every corner of their dwelling, making it a true reflection of the family within. "I wanted the house to look like home," she says. "If you fill your house with only things that you love and things that have meaning to you, it's going to reflect who you are. Every room tells who we are and where we came from. It's our story."

As in the rest of the residence, the soothing master bedroom bears beautiful remembrances of the past. The bed was made with boards from Bob's grandfather's barn, and the vintage window that hangs above was salvaged from the old Indian Land High School that Bob attended before the building was torn down. "There's history of the house and this community in just about every room," Leslie says.

New Victorian Era

WITH PLENTY OF IMAGINATION, INGENUITY, AND ELEGANT FLAIR, ATLANTA
SHOP OWNERS TAKE ON THE IMMENSE CHALLENGE OF TRANSFORMING
A NOTHING-SPECIAL MIDCENTURY IN THE GEORGIA COUNTRYSIDE INTO A
TURN-OF-THE-CENTURY HOME FOR THE NEW MILLENNIUM.

efore this polished duo got ahold of their rural Georgia home, it was more late-midcentury mod than sophisticated classic. Now, the magnificent result of their design aplomb presides over the countryside with courtly grace.

Dan Belman and Randy Korando, partners and proprietors of Boxwoods Gardens and Gifts, carved out a corner of elegance at their shop in the stylish Atlanta neighborhood of Buckhead. But they often found themselves longing for a getaway far from the heavy traffic and bustle of city life. "It is just the two of us, but we have numerous pets, and even more friends, so we wanted to have a second home where we could relax, entertain, and escape the craziness of the big city," says Dan. "We settled on Madison, Georgia, because besides it being a great little town, we like to think of it as one hour and 50 years away from Atlanta."

The gentlemen had their hearts set on something historic with plenty of character, but their search proved more difficult than they had initially imagined. "We originally tried to find an old home with charm and land, but one that wasn't right on the road so we could have privacy and safety for our dogs," says Dan. Undeterred, they settled for something completely unexpected—a midcentury plain Jane with well-hidden potential. "We bought a late 1970s ranch house with the perfect setting and then went about creating what now looks like an 1880s three-story farmhouse by repurposing many old and antique architectural elements."

To look at the home (affectionately dubbed "Camp Boxwoods" by the pair) with its lavish spaces, ornate detailing, and well-established landscape, you would never guess it had such

Stately vaulted ceilings and extensive architectural details leave no trace of the house that Dan and Randy first saw. The ornate is slightly subdued by a quietly clean color palette, allowing the intricacies of the textures and detailing to take center stage. Neutral upholstered furnishings are juxtaposed against fine wood pieces and stunning light fixtures for dramatic effect. There's no shortage of the unique and lovely in the extensive collection of artwork, artifacts, and knickknacks housed here.

humble beginnings. "The majority of the layout is still the same, and we didn't add much to the footprint of the house," explains Dan. But while the home may not have grown out, it certainly grew up. "Low ceilings were our main obstacle, but by removing the original roof before adding two stories on top, we were able to raise the original ceiling heights throughout the main floor," he says.

Like their shop, the home is full of an eclectic mix of old and new, vintage and verdant. "Randy is all about form over function where Dan is the opposite," the couple says. "But after being together for over 30 years, we have learned to listen to each other's ideas and blend both mind-sets for the best results." Each detail in the home has a particular history or sentimental story, too. "Our shop was without question our best source for everything from hardware to furniture to the plates on the wall. As our business entails traveling overseas on buying trips for the store, we have been able to

collect a number of unusual and cherished collections," they note. "Our collections range from simple things like antique scissors to things as fancy as bronze statues."

Some of the most-used rooms of this picket-fenced paradise aren't inside at all. "Adding the five different porches gave us additional spaces for everything from entertaining to sleeping to reading or to do absolutely nothing at all," Dan says of their extensive outdoor living areas. "We also have a large outdoor fire pit, an outdoor shower, which we love, as well as two ponds that we actually swim in."

Every aspect of this vacation escape is impeccably designed, but even more than style, Dan and Randy were aiming for a welcoming spirit in their home. They say, "We would like to believe that Camp Boxwoods offers visitors a warm and friendly home-away-from-home where everybody is just one big happy family."

The kitchen is home to many country farmhouse features with a uniquely French flair. The ceiling, one of the many statement-making features of the home, consists of distressed planks with larger pieces of dark wood in the corners and molding. The backsplash is a gorgeous stone, while the vent hood features an ornate piece of woodwork.

Equestrians at heart, the couple was adamant that the stables on the property housed just as much character and charm as their renovated ranch house. With a towering green-roofed barn and stall doors with unique circular cutouts, these horses are riding in style.

Cloverfield Farm

DESIGNED AS A PLACE TO FIND RESPITE FROM THE FAST PACE OF
CITY LIFE, THIS HOME BREATHES THE WARMTH AND WELCOMING
SPIRIT THAT ONLY COUNTRY LIVING CAN BRING.

W e wanted to build a home that was fitting for the setting," says Jessica Carnell of the barn-style home she and her husband, Kevin, built on 180 acres of land in Tennessee. Dubbed Cloverfield Farm, the home is a treasure trove of reclaimed materials, layered textures, and rich tones that combine to create a comfortable, welcoming space for visitors, no matter how long the stay.

And the Carnells wanted friends and family to be able to stay as long as they liked. Because the home is secluded in the country, far from any store, providing space for everything needed for extended visits was paramount, as was creating an atmosphere that felt far removed from the stress of the city.

To that end, the interior of the home is laden with layers of texture in the form of rich wood planking, rough stone, and a stained concrete floor. "I wanted it to be comfortable and easygoing," Jessica says. Inspired by a country lifestyle, the weathered finishes and darker tones were selected to guard against accidental stains and help nicks and scratches blend in. The elements serve a dual purpose, making a standout statement while helping guests reach complete relaxation.

Large, open spaces were a priority for the couple, and the home's gambrel roof helped fulfill that desire, creating soaring ceilings for the living and dining areas. The open-concept design includes a kitchen that's open to the living space, allowing guests to flow from room to room.

According to Jessica, however, it's often difficult to get them to leave the 10x5-foot island that anchors the kitchen space. "That's usually where everyone gravitates," she says. "As soon as they get to the house, everyone just hangs out in there, and we have to force ourselves to leave and enjoy the other areas."

Reclaimed wood from the military depot in Memphis was used throughout the home, as were materials found on the land. An old wooden post discovered on the property was given new life as the living room mantel. Kevin worked with a local blacksmith to create the double-ring chandeliers in the living area.

Overhead, Thomas O'Brien pendant lights hang from natural wood beams that punctuate a white paneled ceiling. The bank of windows over the sink, painted a dark tone to contrast with the surrounding white, provides an unforgettable view of the surrounding landscape. "We've got a beautiful backdrop," Jessica says. "We wanted to utilize it and bring as much of that from the outside in, so we've got lots of windows on all sides."

Throughout the home, Jessica's inclination to choose texture over color is easily observed. Layers of fabrics featuring varied textures, subtle patterns that range from stripes to florals, and natural elements rich with visual interest blend to create an overall style that lacks nothing for its shortage of bright tones. "I'm more of a muted person," Jessica says. She changes out pillows, throws, and other textiles as the seasons change, decorating with lighter linens in the summer and preparing for winter's chill with heavier fabrics.

With an emphasis on making guests feel at home, the bedroom spaces are no exception to the home's refined rustic style. The iron bed that tops a sisal rug in one guest room has an added element of coziness provided by an upholstered headboard, and a mixture of stripes and solids pile the bed with comfort. The brightest spot in the room, the floral curtains are juxtaposed with the weathered wooden finish of the dresser that serves as a nightstand.

Attached to the rear of the home, the screened-in gazebo is a favorite of homeowners and visitors alike. "We play a lot of card games and board games out there and look at the pond," Jessica says. "We started a vineyard earlier, and so it's nice to see that all coming together." The space is warmed not only by the stone fireplace, but also by rich wood planking and seating options layered with textures and gray tones. But possibly its most breathtaking feature is the natural landscaping that surrounds it, reminding those inside just what farmhouse living is all about.

Opposite: Even in lighter spaces, such as the bunk room, an abundance of textures creates a feeling of coziness. Planked walls contrast with the mirrored surface and curved detailing of the dresser, and varied patterns on the bed linens add a touch of warmth.

Close to Home

THOUGH THIS FAMILY OF THREE DESIRED SPACES OF THEIR OWN
AND HAD PLENTY OF LAND TO ACCOMODATE THEM, A COZY,
COMFORTABLE FARMHOUSE TENDS TO BRING THEM ALL TOGETHER.

The property, affectionately named Nestledown, was originally planned to be a commercial development, but the homeowners fell in love with the land and location and decided to make it their home. A true equestrian's paradise, the home features a massive barn right next to riding rings and pastures for the horses to graze in.

With over 15 acres of land to live on, this family had more than enough room to spread out. But they had one request of the builder, John Bynum—to be close together. "They'd had their home, barn, and office miles away from each other before, so they really wanted to have the home, the dream barn, and the lake house all together on one piece of property," John recalls.

With a mother-daughter equestrian team, the property has no shortage of amenities for the riders, including paddocks, pastures, and riding rings. Echoing the country scenery and the homeowner's lifestyle, the main house, barn, and lake house all share complementing farmhouse-style exteriors, with white planked walls and black doors and window frames. But the interiors of each structure have their own style, each exploring a different facet of country living.

The main house, designed by architect Peter Quinn with the homeowner's lifestyle in mind, features an elegant take on farmhouse style, with a statement-making lighting fixture and arched ceiling in the entryway. True to country style, rustic touches like shiplap and brick flooring bring the whole space down to earth.

The kitchen carries the black and white theme, with rich hardwood floors adding a little bit of color to the space. Though the homeowners only have one child, they opted for an abundance of seating for when family and friends gather in the space, as they often do. The kitchen leads into a breakfast nook, anchored by an ornate Oriental rug and rustic brick fireplace. The dining room also sits right off the kitchen and has a wall of windows that allows natural light to pour in.

Hardwood floors and shiplap walls continue into the living room, but splashes of color are introduced with a blue-and-white printed coffee table, royal blue arm chairs, and pops of orange in accent pillows. Floor-to-ceiling windows bring in the scenery. Pops of orange and blue also make an appearance in the daughter's room. Decorated with winning competition ribbons, the space is anchored by another Oriental rug and bohemian blue-and-white bedding.

The homeowner's master suite takes a more serene approach, with heavy drapery and coordinating bed linens and dusty blue accents. At the foot of the room sits a fireplace that makes for extra cozy evenings in the winter. The bathroom houses an elegant claw-foot tub next to windows with a gorgeous view of the property, as well as double vanities.

Though the main house shines with its elegant take on farmhouse style, the husband might consider the crown jewel of the property to be the lake house, a structure that he and John designed on a whim. The home has a loft-like atmosphere, with a completely open floor plan and industrial style. Instead of continuing the familiar shiplap, John opted for brick walls that complement the wood-beamed ceiling and exposed ductwork.

With a main house, lake house, and barn, it's safe to say that each member of the household has their own personal space. But, at the end of the day, togetherness is always the priority in this home.

The kitchen takes a retreat from the pops of color seen in other living spaces around the house. Ceiling-height subway tile complements the equally high cabinetry. Though the upper cabinets extend many feet high, John and the homeowners kept the space cozy by sectioning off the cabinets, with the lower part being traditional doors, the middle glass-fronted, and the top an extended crown molding. These features, added with the island lighting fixtures, draw the eye upward to notice the gorgeous white planked ceiling.

The couple's adult daughter, also an award-winning equestrian like her mother, has a space of her own when she visits her parent's farmhouse. Distinctly mature, the room also has an air of fun, thanks to the bright orange and blue color palette and the bold prints used. The space is full of nostalgic touches, like ribbons and treasured stuffed animals to truly make the room feel like home.

In the master suite, notes of nature reign supreme. John, Peter, and the homeowners used the same sectioning concept they did with the kitchen cabinetry with the master bedroom windows, with a break in between the bottom and top pieces of glass. Floor-to-ceiling drapes keep the space grounded and cozy as well. The multitude of windows next to rich touches of natural wood in the floors and roman shades, in addition to pastoral printed pillows and drapes in the bathroom, all tie the outdoors inside the suite.

In addition to the lake house, the husband also has a study, complete with dark gray walls, a gun cabinet, wine storage, and a private entrance.

Cottage to Farmhouse

PRESERVING A SMALLER PROPERTY NEAR THE
CITY, THIS HOME LIES PERPENDICULAR TO THE
PROPERTY, OFFERING A FRONTAL VIEW THAT
FEELS SMALLER TO SUIT THE NEIGHBORHOOD.

This small, 1940s cottage was redesigned as a farmhouse for a family of five. Centrally located in a small town, the desire was to blend into the community setting. By planning the renovation to rest on the property in a vertical manner, the home appears to blend with other homes of varying size surrounding it. Designers Sunni Glidewell and Pandy Agnew, along with architect Jordan Hostetler, utilized plenty of reclaimed wood from floor to ceiling to breathe new life into the design and to salvage a sense of the historic cottage within its walls. Nestled on the lot, the shadow box fencing borders a private garden and pool area in the rear of the property. A covered porch is partially screened for additional privacy to dine off the family room. Plenty of windows allow light to spill into the home, adding a floor-to-ceiling spaciousness to the interior. Additional windows added over the kitchen counters enhance the cook's view.

The home was designed to accommodate plenty of entertaining space for family in its central great room, kitchen, and gathering rooms. A wide entry hall opens up to greet guests, alongside the generous dining room, filled with an heirloom table and French sideboard. Use of antique finds, such as door panels with iron insets, create farmhouse touches in the interior. Family activity rooms abound upstairs—one above the family room allows for children to entertain friends, while another over the garage area is for viewing sports or enjoying a game of billiards.

The use of color is limited to allow a fresh look with emphasis on reclaimed areas of the home. Simplicity and restraint allow a punch of color sparingly in curtains throughout the home.

All in all, a two-story home with additional depth provided these homeowners the opportunity to keep the old setting, preserving most of the existing wood within a modern farmhouse for all of their tomorrows.

Opposite: The vaulted, two-story family room is focused on the fireplace area. A wall of French doors lights the room on the left, while a framed mirrored wall piece brightens the opposite wall. An arch of collected turquoise plates adds a splash of color.

Thoughtful space planning ensured ample counterspace and corner light desired by the homeowners. A large island topped with sparkling white marble creates plenty of serving and prep space. The dining table in the gathering room looks over the garden area, with orange-and-turquoise patterned curtains adding color to the room. Bookcase niches display kitchen collectibles, while the tin light fixture adds interest to a table grouping of various chairs and a side bench.

In the kitchen, natural tones are paired with soft gray hues to create a sophisticated space with a hint of rustic style. The patterned tile of the backsplash extends to the ceiling, where rich wooden beams add an extra layer of character.

Soft sunlight warms a work area tucked behind a set of weathered French doors. Wooden shelves provide space for organization while contributing to the honeyed tones in the space, and a rug and throw pillow introduce a touch of color and comfort.

Opposite: The crossbeam designed ceiling is the focal point for a large, polished marble chandelier. The calm coloration of the bedding adds comfort and beauty along with the soft green draperies flanking the windows.

Californian Charm

INSPIRED BY A LOVE OF FRENCH FARMHOUSE STYLE, THIS HOMEOWNER BREATHED NEW LIFE INTO HER HISTORIC HOME.

of "a fresh coat of everything," Lizzie says. Deena addressed the problem with an abundance of white paint, which she used on the planked walls and ceilings as well as the furniture itself. "Most of my furniture is white, and if it isn't, it's got something white over it," she notes. "It's just something I love, and I feel like it's very farmhouse."

The bright and airy backdrop lends itself to the cozy, casual style seen in the furnishings and accents throughout the home, and the neutral palette allows an easy marrying of weathered finishes, plush chairs, and country-style linens. Where color has been introduced, it is restricted to cheerful, calming shades that are complemented by the glow of the sunlight pouring in from the home's many windows. "When you look at the French world or European farm lifestyle, it's very clean," Deena says. The designer notes that farmhouse style often features wooden textures, green foliage, and lots of white. "So those are kind of where I try to go," she says.

In addition to infusing the home with a breath of fresh air, Deena had to make a few improvements to the amenities. While the kitchen came with a number of updated features, including butcher block countertops, she opted to replace the shallow, narrow sink with a deeper model and give the entire room the same bright-white treatment. Upstairs, Deena's attic bedroom, which was once dark and cave-like, can now be likened to a cozy, fairytale-esque sanctuary. New laminate flooring sporting a weathered finish replaced the old carpeting, and relaxed white furniture sets the scene for a tranquil respite. Details like the carved edge of the desk Deena brought with her from Santa Monica, California, are the finishing touches needed to make the space really feel special.

Recently, Deena went through the process of having the farmhouse declared a historical landmark, one of the many ways she has tried to honor the home's heritage. Throughout the design process, she strove to create a style that was "in keeping with what the bones of the house were," she says. She accomplished that goal through her generous use of light tones and layered textures and, in the process, gave new life to a home that truly deserved it.

D esigner Deena Benz has always had a deep appreciation for farmhouse style. So when she had the opportunity to purchase her own farmhouse in Los Olivos, California, she jumped at the chance. "It was a very happy accident how I found this place," Deena says of the structure, which was built in 1886 and originally belonged to influential early members of the community. "It's a very special place to me. I'm just so grateful it chose me."

At the time of the purchase in 2014, Deena was the owner of Farmhouse Goods, a home décor business formed in collaboration with interior designer, shop owner, and friend Lizzie McGraw, whom Deena calls her inspiration. Both women's styles—and inventories—played a part in revitalizing the home's interior, but it was ultimately Deena's love of light that transformed the space into what it is today.

Originally laden with dark wood tones, gloomy greens, and outdated carpeting, the cottage was in desperate need

COTTAGE RULES
WAKE UP SMILING
SOAK UP THE SUN
BUILD SAND CASTLES
CATCH THE WAVES
EAT SOME SEAFOOD
TAKE LONG WALKS
ENJOY THE OCEAN BREEZE
LOOK FOR SHELLS
FLIP FLOPS MANDATORY
NAP DAILY HAVE FUN

The dining area is the perfect gathering place for friends and family. The farm table is complemented by a set of chairs Deena painted and sanded. Turkish towels serve as window treatments, and the bench is made cozy by an assortment of grain sack pillows.

Once filled with dark woods, the kitchen is now a reflection of Deena's light and airy style, and a splash of aqua blue breathes vibrancy into the space.

The expanse of white in Deena's bedroom reflects the glow of the California sun, creating a serene backdrop for the dashes of pink and turquoise found throughout the space.

Storied Style
on the Lake

HISTORIC CHARM ABOUNDS IN THIS FARMHOUSE
HIDDEN AWAY IN A SLEEPY SOUTHERN HAMLET.

Upon first glance, Debra and Todd Turner's farmhouse, nestled on 600 acres of land in Fitzpatrick, Alabama, looks like a glimpse into the past. With weathered wooden siding enriched by cheerful red doors and shutters, the home is a picture of warm, rustic style reminiscent of days gone by. But despite its nostalgic appearance, the home was built fewer than 10 years ago.

"We wanted to design a home that would look like it had been there for 100 years," explains Debra. To execute their vision, she and her husband, Todd, hired architect Keith Summerour, who drew up plans for a dogtrot house. Featuring an open breezeway with sleeping spaces on one side and cooking and living spaces on the other, the style was popular throughout the Southeastern United States during the 19th and early 20th centuries. "So, that was the architectural style that we wanted to replicate," Debra says.

Inside, Keith worked with designers Stephanie Geyer and Melanie Millner to craft a space that welcomes every guest with cozy, historic style. "We wanted it to look authentically period," Debra says. "So that's why we looked for the rustic beams and ceiling, and the hardwood floor was reclaimed out of a factory in Georgia that was built in the late 1800s."

Adding to the earthy, textured charm of the house, the walls were planked with boards in a variety of widths. A milk paint finish adorns the walls of the living room and kitchen, brightening the space without obscuring the grain of the wood beneath. When it came to shopping for furniture, antiques markets and salvage stores were scoured for pieces possessing the perfect character. "The island in the kitchen came from an old mechanic's shop," Debra points out, adding that it's perfect for storing their collection of cast-iron skillets and their supplies for entertaining. "It's so efficient."

While, historically, dogtrot houses feature an open breezeway, the farmhouse's middle section was enclosed with metal-and-glass doors to house the dining room. Warmed by a potbelly stove next to a brick-sided staircase, the space features a pecky cypress farm table that seats 16. "Our big focus is hosting family gatherings," Debra says. "We just wanted to make it very comfortable, where any guest who would come would feel like they didn't want to leave."

Because Debra and Todd's two children were in college while the house was being designed, they incorporated two master bedrooms on the main floor and 10 bunk beds upstairs. "We wanted a home that could expand and contract, depending on how many people were visiting us," Debra says. The upstairs design also includes a washer and dryer, shower, and changing area, and has accommodated as many as 10 college students comfortably.

No matter who is staying over, you can always find someone relaxing on the back porch, which looks down to the lake and is Debra and Todd's favorite part of the home. "Even when the weather's hot, we're there watching people swim in the lake and then dry off on the porch. And in the wintertime, it's the perfect place to watch all the geese come in," Debra says. "We have our coffee there every morning."

In every corner—inside and out—the design's dedication to historic style fills this farmhouse with rich, comforting style. No matter the time of year, the home's country-style hospitality warmly welcomes all who enter.

The mantel is made of wood salvaged from Debra's family farm in Pennsylvania, which was built in the 1700s. "We were able to salvage the timbers from this old implement shed," Debra says, "so, we were excited to ship them down to Alabama and incorporate them." A collection of antlers atop the wood is a nod to the area's abundant deer hunting.

A gorgeously detailed English hutch purchased from Scott Antique Markets in Atlanta, Georgia, houses the family's china, which features nature-inspired images like deer and hunting fowl. "We use them all the time—they're not just for show," Debra notes. "That's the china we use to eat on." On the wall, a sconce created from an antique flour tin provides a touch of weathered interest.

The tobacco-stick broom on the wall of the kitchen is something that Debra likes to point out. "I grew up in Virginia, and I worked in tobacco—most people don't even know what a tobacco stick is," she says. "In the original days of curing tobacco, they would hang the tobacco off these sticks."

In one of the downstairs bedrooms, the red cast-iron bed is the perfect touch of farmhouse charm. "The quilt on top of that is my husband's great-grandmother's quilt that she hand-stitched," Debra says.

The popular back porch features a daybed, bent hickory chairs, and a table that seats ten. In addition to the farmhouse, the land features a barn, stables, a bass lake, and more. The farm is home to black angus cows, horses, and 20 beehives.

The Honeymoon Home

NEARLY 15 YEARS AFTER BUILDING A RUSTIC
CARRIAGE HOUSE FOR HIS NEW BRIDE,
DANNY MCEACHERN NOW LETS OTHER NEWLYWEDS
LIVE OUT THEIR WEDDING DREAMS IN THE HOME

After graduating from college with a degree in architecture from Auburn University, Danny McEachern was sure his future consisted of designing homes and buildings. And it did for a decade, including the carriage house he built as a newlywed on his family's land outside of Gadsden, Alabama. With a passion for good design, it was no surprise that he crafted a masterpiece. Inspired by the design of cottages at one of the couple's favorite destinations, Rosemary Beach, Florida, the home's arched entryways and eaves for the roof give a taste of the rustic beauty inside.

Within the first few steps, proof of Danny's persistence and devotion to design is evident. Though the home was built less than two decades ago, it has a vintage atmosphere and patina of age that makes it seem as though it has always existed on the family farm. Danny meticulously resourced every piece in the home to achieve the perfect balance of classic and modern style. Many of the furnishings in the home are antique, but even the pieces that aren't are so expertly crafted to resemble vintage furniture that it's almost impossible to distinguish them from the rest.

Nowadays, the carriage house has new life but with a similar purpose. Nearly a decade ago, Danny and his wife decided to open what they then thought would be a side business as a wedding venue on their property. But after 50 weddings in their first season, they quickly realized the potential of the locale, and Danny left his architecture career to devote his full attention to the wedding business. Not long afterward, the couple built a new home and gave their quaint carriage house a renewed sense of purpose as a bridal suite and honeymoon cottage.

On almost any given weekend throughout the year, the carriage house is caught in the hustle and bustle of wedding preparations, but there's no better place to do so. Not surprisingly, Danny's wife's favorite feature is also the most popular with the new brides—the master bathroom. With a vintage claw-foot tub next to an arched doorway overlooking the grounds, the spot was a must-have when building and is now a bonus relaxation spot for brides.

While the carriage house might be small, with vaulted ceilings over 20 feet high and a practical, open-concept flow, it's able to handle the chaos with ease. The cozy kitchen features a wooden island and offers additional space with a bar. Flowing into the living room, the crown jewel of the home is showcased—the antique mantel. A quick trip up the stairs reveals the welcoming master loft. Nestled under the eaves and behind effervescent white drapes is a cozy queen bed, perfect for newlyweds.

Though it's been nearly 10 years since the couple moved out of the cottage, Danny admits that he still misses it from time to time. But he takes comfort in knowing that his perfect honeymoon suite lives on to provide the same joy to couples from across the nation.

In addition to the carriage house, the McEachern's farm also includes a barn, stables, and an apple orchard that are available for weddings.

While the kitchen of the home was originally where Danny and his wife lovingly prepared meals for each other, it now acts as a spot for friends and family to gather with a bride and groom before their big day. Danny recalls skepticism from others when he mentioned including two islands, but now anyone who sees the space admits that it works perfectly well.

132

Opposite the quaint bedroom loft area is a charming window bench overlooking the grounds. The spot offers a place of respite during one of the busiest seasons of a young couple's life together. The bed is nestled in the coziest spot of the cottage, under eaves of natural wood and hidden by soft, dreamy curtains.

Another must-have on Danny's list was an extensive garden. He admits his passion for the hobby, even growing the majority of the family's produce in their own backyard.

Modern Country Style

TRADITIONAL FARMHOUSE MEETS ON-TREND STYLE, AND SOMETHING
BEAUTIFUL HAPPENS. THIS CANADIAN COUNTRY HOME HAS ENVIABLE INDIVIDUALITY AND CHARM.

When Robin and Robert Ogilvie decided to buy a weekend home, they had no idea how many surprises, twists, and turns their journey would take—or that they would achieve their very own happily ever after.

It's hard to believe that this house is actually a new build. The stunning timber beams and stone walls evoke a bygone era more akin to the original settlement on this large 116-acre piece of land in Caledon, Ontario. But when Robin and Robert first came to view the property, it wasn't at all what they were looking for. Perhaps the real estate agent who brought them here guessed that it was just right for the couple who were, at the time, just looking for a property for the weekends that included a barn for Robin's two horses. They lived and worked in Toronto at the time, so a huge project was not a desirable option for them.

Originally settled in 1904, Coffey Creek Farm incorporated a large 100-year-old barn and a rather

run-down, unimpressive 1970s farmhouse that would need a lot of work to bring it up to the low-maintenance standard the couple hoped for. Robin was keen to put their stamp and style onto any property they found that needed a bit of work and redecorating, but any thoughts of building their own house couldn't have been further from their minds.

As soon as they saw the property and the stunning land and views surrounding them, the couple began to plan a way to make it work. Quite rightly, Robert saw a great investment opportunity, and there was more than enough land for Robin's horses, but the house itself was uninspiring. They bought it, and before they knew it, they had chosen a site on the land, up high to benefit from the best possible views, and they were speaking with architects.

"We asked three separate architects to come up with plans for a stone house with European and local influences. Surprisingly, the youngest, least experienced of them came up with the best design," says Robin. And so Wayne Swadron was employed for the Ogilvie house build. "Apparently, he had never even been to a farm or a house like it, and yet his design felt perfect in every way, as if it had been here for generations," Robin explains. "We worked together every step of the way, and it evolved." Much of the inspiration came from magazines, often sourced by Robin's friends. "They sent me magazines from Europe—garden and home mags—and I would tear pages out and show them to Wayne."

Importantly, the build incorporated local materials—just as it would have done on that same land back in the early 1900s—so the stone for the walls, including the hallways, dining room, and living room, all came from the local quarry. The beautiful beams that look so well aged do so for a reason: They were all reclaimed from local decommissioned barns. The timber floorboards were also salvaged from within a few miles of the house.

Wayne designed the house in the style of a European country manor. There is the main house, spread over two floors, and an additional single-level property that appears to have been added on but was in fact built at the same time, which they call the bungalow. The bungalow houses the kitchen and dining area with an adjacent sitting room and the master bedroom. "We also wanted a guest suite, and Wayne came up with a stunning arched walkway connecting

us to where our children and grandchildren stay when they visit," Robin says. "Wayne really liked the idea of making the main house look older than the bungalow, so he chose to use different materials and styles for the different spaces. It works perfectly." The guest wing resembles a barn, in keeping with the rural location. "The guest rooms have been panelled, and this has instantly given it a more modern feel than the exposed stone walls in the main house and bungalow," she says.

As for décor and furnishings, Robin began by sticking to the farmhouse style and filled the house with traditional furniture. However, as time went by, she enjoyed mixing it up with some more modern midcentury items. The combination of old and new, traditional and quirky, gives the house a style of its own. There are fantastic texture and material combinations, including the use of exposed copper pipes on the sink that, against the exposed pale stone, feels

almost like you're in a New York industrial loft apartment. The palette throughout allows the building itself to be the center of attention. The stone walls and wooden beams are the stars of the show, ensuring you don't forget this is a country house. There are constant hints to the past and location, as well as touches that speak of modernity and city life. This house feels timeless, as if it's been in the family for generations.

The entire process from purchase to full build took two years. Within that time there was a huge transformation, not only in the building, but for both Robin and Robert, who realized that they had something very special here on this land. So special, in fact, that they decided to sell their Toronto home and move here full-time. Their weekend retreat became their home.

And it really has changed their lives—Robin now breeds and trains Rocky and Kentucky Mountain horses for a living.

Opposite: A wonderful green rug contrasts with everything else—the beautiful, large family table, dark pine floors, and iron chandelier.

Salvaged timber beams frame the open shelving that displays uninterrupted glassware. The pullout storage drawers are wide and ensure that practicality and efficiency remain key to the overall design.

Robin has given this room warmth and style with lots of texture with shaggy pillows paired with woven and knitted throws.

The Beauty of the Earth

ORIGINALLY INTENDED TO BE A TEMPORARY HOME, THIS RENOVATED BARN TURNED OUT TO BE THE IDEAL PLACE FOR A GROWING FAMILY TO PUT DOWN PERMANENT ROOTS.

Back when Michelle and Kelly Colbert's stunning farmhouse was a simple brown cedar barn, they fell in love with the land around it. "They loved the property," says interior designer Ashley Gilbreath, "and they were going to build their forever house on another location on the property." In the meantime, the Colberts hired architect Andy Smith to renovate the existing barn house into a temporary living space.

And then, he started drawing. "We had no idea of the options, and all of a sudden, he drew this humongous dormer where he made the whole house go out eight feet upstairs," says Michelle. It was the beginning of the realization that there might be more to the structure than met the eye. Space above the barn provided much-needed room for the family, and it wasn't long before they made the decision to transform the barn into a home fit for generations of Colberts to come.

With the transformation now complete, the resulting farmhouse features bright white shiplap walls complemented by cheery pastels and enriched with natural wood elements. "I just wanted everything really calm and pretty," says Michelle, noting that her previous home featured a lot of bolder hues. She and Ashley achieved the desired look through the use of blush pink tones and a range of blue shades which, when paired with the clean white of the walls and furniture and the honeyed tone of the arched ceiling beams, create the cozy feel of home.

And making the farmhouse feel like home was a must for Michelle and Kelly, who needed plenty of room for their five children, as well as future grandchildren. "She wanted tons of counter stools," Ashley says of Michelle. "She wanted a table that stretched if needed and additional chairs to pull up, but to also have overflow space and a seating room."

Making the home livable was another priority, not only because of a large family but also because of the dozens of animals that live on the land—and sometimes in the house. Dogs, cats, goats, chickens, and more often spend time inside with the family, which meant that Ashley needed to utilize materials that were durable and beautiful. Sunbrella fabrics, treated surfaces, and indoor/outdoor rugs helped her create a design that could be lived in but still exuded the feeling that Michelle wanted.

"She wanted to reinvent the feeling that she got when she walked into her grandmother's house," Ashley says. Through the use of antique pieces, weathered finishes, and cozy textures, they recreated the welcoming warmth of Michelle's childhood memories while avoiding an outdated vibe. Vintage quilts draped across spool beds in one bedroom not only provide a soft touch of color in an airy space but also create texture and warmth. In one son's room, a family heirloom serves as a headboard, and an antique bench from a shop in Belgium sits at the foot of the master bed. "We played with mixing elements and using that patina of a more 'loved-on' finish rather than everything being brand new," Ashley adds.

In the end, the property that drew the Colberts to the home became an integral part of the design. Banks of windows provide daily views of both the morning sunrise and the sunset over the lake, and a sunroom with four sets of folding doors is the perfect place to entertain and enjoy the vibrancy of the natural landscape. "It's just beautiful," Michelle says of the view. "And for me, that was the focal point—even more so than the artwork or anything—just being able to see the outside."

A rough-hewn wooden beam over the stove range injects a level of warmth and earthy charm into the kitchen, contrasting with the white shiplap above and the patterned tile backsplash below. A collection of European mounts is a nod to the family's love of hunting. The kitchen space features a number of antique pieces, including a pommel horse recovered from a gym in Europe that serves as a bench.

Opposite: The four-poster bed in the master bedroom was custom made for Michelle and Kelly by Reid Classics.

A bunk room upstairs provides a place for the family to gather and watch movies or simply spend time together. A loft overhead holds another sleeping space complete with a queen-size bed.

The youngest daughter's bedroom pairs feminine, contemporary elements with vintage pieces such as the nightstands, which were used in a hospital in Europe during one of the world wars.

The Good Life

SET AMIDST A SCENIC COUNTRY LANDSCAPE IN NOTTAWA, ONTARIO, AND JUST A SHORT DRIVE FROM THE PULSATING CITY OF TORONTO, A MODERN FARMHOUSE PROVIDES THE PERFECT ESCAPE TO A SIMPLER LIFE FOR THIS CANADIAN FAMILY.

When the former home on the property was torn down, the old barn was stripped to the studs and rebuilt on its original site. Surrounded by low-maintenance boxwood hedges, the new barn provides a charming focal point from the main house. The barn, which includes a hay loft up top, has housed many animals, such as miniature donkeys, rabbits, ducks, goats, and a horse. For its next life, Wispy wants to renovate the barn to create a pool house.

The farm lifestyle was always "the dream" for Canadian couple Wispy Boivin and her husband, Christophe. It was with this vision in mind that they packed up their family and left Toronto behind. Their new life awaited within the small hamlet of Nottawa, Ontario, an idyllic setting just five minutes from Collingwood and Town of The Blue Mountains—a scenic four-season area known for its ski hills and beautiful Georgian Bay waterfronts.

"Moving out of the city has been the best decision we have ever made," says Wispy, a real estate professional and yoga instructor. "The kids can roam free around the property, ski after school, use the bay, and hike in the summer. We also love our downtime and love having our own retreat away from neighbors," she adds.

It took five years of being in this sublime setting and trying out a house by the water, in town, close to town, and around neighbors with kids before Wispy and her husband finally found the farm they both knew was the perfect fit. Although it was built in 2009, the house has many antique doors and vintage hardware to create that rustic original farmhouse look and feel. White siding and traditional white windows provide a decidedly clean and modern look, along with a white board-and-batten garage and an addition featuring black windows and accents. With only eight-foot-high ceilings, it was a challenge to make the house look as open and bright as possible. Painting the orange pine floors and walls bright white really helped to achieve this.

"It's not hard to see that my go-to is to paint everything I see white," jokes Wispy. "Nothing is safe—walls, furniture, floors— but I do love splashes of color, interest in fabrics and wallpaper, and the wonderful textures of salvaged pieces that I continue to find and collect," she adds.

In the great room, Wispy had to have 11-foot ceilings and oversize windows. Adding color, large sofas and rugs, bookshelves, and a piano befit the grand scale of the space and gave it a warm, lived-in feel. Used mostly as a family room, this inviting area is where all the kids pile in, watch movies, play the piano, and listen to old records.

Accented with vibrant blue accessories and awash in bright white paint—homeowner Wispy Boivin's self-professed signature mark—the great room takes on a decidedly clean, contemporary feel. Reclaimed bricks embedded in the fireplace wall balance the modernity with a refined, rustic elegance. A whimsical feather chandelier is one of Wispy's favorite home furnishings. She admits to excluding it from every house sale, and it moves with her no matter what.

"We entertain a lot in this room after dinner," says Wispy. "The large silk rug anchors the room and creates a sense of warmth and interest. I like the plush softness and the playfulness of the pattern," she adds.

The kitchen is another favorite hangout, where the family enjoys spending time together cooking, eating meals, and catching up on the day. Highly functional and equipped with state-of-the-art appliances, this bright white space emits a decidedly relaxed vibe. An adjoining sitting area features a large trestle table that Wispy whitewashed with a high-gloss spray paint, as well as her coveted collection of mismatched vintage chairs. A Rumford fireplace makes the space warm and alluring both day and night, especially in winter.

"I really don't know the technicalities of design, but for me, the white paint obviously plays a big role," laughs Wispy. "I just want to make sure everything in my home has meaning and creates a certain feeling that makes you want to be in the space. I think it's important to stay true to your style, even if you can't define what that is," she notes.

An active family to say the least, Wispy and Christophe tend to their many passions daily. With one or two restaurants to manage, as well as yoga sessions and a nonstop career in renovating and selling houses, the Boivins have made moving from home to home an adventure they embrace. The kids know how to pack, redecorate their rooms, and get acquainted with their new surroundings. They meditate together often and always have a house full of kids and friends up from the city. Feeding the animals, running around freely, gathering eggs and fresh vegetables, cooking, and snuggling in by the fire are blissful family pastimes the farm lifestyle has provided them.

"It has been everything we dreamed it would be," says Wispy. "We wake up early and walk the dogs through the back trails in our pajamas while we walk toward the sun as it rises. The kids call it sun-chaser mornings, and it does something to my soul in these moments."

The all-white kitchen emits a sleek, modern vibe and offers the perfect backdrop for warm farmhouse-style finishes such as brass hardware for the kitchen sink, painted pine floors, and the black barn board at the base of the island. A gleaming overhead light is actually a vintage bowl the homeowners turned upside down and painted the underside gold to complement the brass faucet and hardware. Fresh green accents throughout add a vibrant pop of color while adding homey warmth and charm to this monochromatic space.

A Passion for Preservation

RICH HISTORY AND TIMEWORN STYLE SPILL FROM EVERY
CORNER OF THIS METICULOUSLY RESTORED BARN.

While there aren't many historic homes to be found in Jackson, Wyoming, that didn't stop Shelley and John Holland from finding their own piece of the past to call home. "I grew up identifying with restoration," says John, who spent his childhood visiting a Colonial home that his grandfather saved from flooding prior to the creation of a reservoir in Massachusetts. "It's a little bit in my DNA, I guess."

Driven by heritage and a desire to find something that would be worth their effort, Shelley and John eventually discovered their future home waiting for them in Ontario. "It was in the process of being potentially torn down to put up a large retail store," John says. "So, obviously, we wanted to save the frame."

That frame, which Shelley and John fell in love with, consists of 12x12 beams hand-hewn from northern white pine and was constructed in a way that makes it perfect for the heavy snowfall and seismic activity of the region. Featuring an immense, meticulously crafted swing beam—designed to allow wagons to turn around within the barn—the structure showed the marks of a craftsman who loved his work. "Clearly, he was passionate," John says, "like the Michelangelo of barn building."

Realizing that the structure was the most well-built barn they had seen, the couple decided to preserve the frame as it was. That meant retrofitting a livable space in a way that honored its character and history. "It's quite a bit of work to try to reengineer a house around a frame," John says, quick to add that they happily adapted their lifestyle around it.

And the layout of the barn naturally lent itself to the openness that he and Shelley desired. The kitchen, dining, and living areas flow together, creating a soaring space filled with sunlight from the windows that nearly fill one wall. "Having grown up in very small New England homes, we wanted to take advantage of the volume of this barn to create a great room and openness with broad views and a bigger, open space for us to live in day to day," John says.

He and Shelley also seized the opportunity to take the project in a sustainable direction. "Part of what makes this barn restoration project so appealing is that it's intrinsically green in terms of its approach," John says. Complementing the original frame, other reclaimed materials include the heart pine flooring and exterior siding. Railings and countertops were created from joists that were originally underneath the barn, and American clay is an earthy alternative to paint or paper on the walls. "Everywhere you look, you see reclaimed material inside and out," John says.

In contrast to the spaciousness of the great room, the Hollands were looking for smaller bedroom spaces. "We took advantage of the coziness of the natural partitions to make smaller, more intimate sleeping spaces while preserving that large, open, vaulted feel in the primary living space," John says. Antique quilts and rustic finishes contribute to the warmth of the spaces, as well as imbuing them with the same sense of history that fills every room.

Throughout the home, a collection of antiques includes both family heirlooms and newly acquired pieces—but each with its own history. "My mother was an interior designer, and my father ran an antiques shop in Nantucket, Massachusetts," John says. "We honored the age and the history of the building by furnishing it with a number of hand-me-down antiques that were complementary in terms of having that traditional, authentic, historic feel without making it feel like a museum."

Whether it's the antique English pub settle off the living room or the reclaimed cypress on the master bedroom fireplace that was once used in mushroom cultivation in upstate New York, there isn't a room in the house that doesn't hold a story. Through every step of the restoration process, Shelley and John carefully considered every inch of their one-of-a-kind home, perfectly preserving the past for generations to come.

In reference to the materials used and the care that went into the design, John says that the barn is "truly spectacular," noting that the barnwright "was so passionate that he made a number of improvements to the barn that wouldn't be necessary— that may be more aesthetic—and really put his heart and soul in every barn that he built."

An important element of the rebuilding process for the Hollands was to design the home in a way that—if the need ever arose—the frame could be taken apart piece by piece and transported. "This barn can actually be disassembled and left completely intact the way it was originally built," John says.

Chosen for its character and warmth, the reclaimed cypress that surrounds the master bedroom fireplace was once used in the mushroom industry. "They needed dark spaces and structures that would not rot in terms of the moisture, because they required a very humid environment," John explains. "They actually turned to the South—to the bayous—to find wood that would be able to withstand rotting." Over the fireplace, a personalized topographical map of the region was a gift from John's mother.

Before moving into the barn, the Hollands relocated and restored a log cabin from West Virginia with its own interesting history. "About five rows up, you can see that the structure went from what was originally called a V-notch to just a straight dovetail," John says. Digging into the history, they discovered that the cabin's builders changed after the first team left to join the Civil War and never returned.

Paradise Rebuilt

AFTER A DEVASTATING FIRE DESTROYED THEIR MOUNTAIN HOME,
THESE HOMEOWNERS WORKED WITH THEIR TALENTED NEIGHBORS
TO RECREATE IT—AND THIS TIME BETTER THAN BEFORE.

At first glance, Anne Moore and Bryan Baldwin's rustic retreat is the epitome of living in tranquil harmony with nature. Designed by architect Al Platt and situated in North Carolina, it appears to have always been there—until the homeowners reveal the rest of their story. "We first built the house seven years ago, but in 2011, lightning struck the place and burned it to the ground," Bryan recounts. "It was a total loss."

Many people would have considered moving on, but a chance meeting with nearby neighbors Maxine and Jeff Sikes changed all that. "Jeff and I were concerned that Bryan and Anne wouldn't rebuild," Maxine says. "We had just completed our home in the same neighborhood and couldn't stand the thought of them never returning." As owners of the company Global Reclamations, Maxine and Jeff proved to be the perfect pair for inspiring the Baldwins to reconsider.

Pleased with the architect's original design, the Baldwins determined to build it from scratch once again; but this time they were guided by the know-how of their neighbors. The collaboration resulted in an abode more stunning than its previous version.

Described as "rustic mountain elegance" by the homeowners, the retreat's décor captures an impeccable yet comfortable ambience. It juxtaposes rustic finishes with elegant elements—for example, using pearl quartz countertops in the kitchen alongside reclaimed beams and barn wood. Likewise, they paired limestone in the second master with industrial natural steel vanity bases and skip-planed, heart pine ceilings.

While the spaces throughout the home are lovely on their own, each room offers breathtaking views of the surrounding mountain setting. The house also boasts a series of porches and decks that the Baldwins and their

guests flock to year-round. "In particular, our sunroom is a perfect spot for catching up on reading while enjoying the cool mountain breezes at an elevation of 4,300 feet," Bryan adds.

With their haven re-established, the homeowners take full advantage of it by entertaining friends or relishing its peace and quiet as a family. But whatever the occasion, Anne and Bryan will always be grateful to their neighbors for keeping their dream alive. "Maxine and Jeff put their hearts and souls into building and decorating our house, and we couldn't be more pleased with what they accomplished," Bryan confesses. "As well as being talented neighbors, they're now great friends."

Accented with a coffered ceiling formed from antique beams, the Baldwins' kitchen is conveniently located near a built-in bar area, along with a sunny nook containing a charming breakfast table. "The countertops and backsplash in the kitchen are composed of natural quartzite, and underfoot, the reclaimed, heart pine flooring displays a subtle shimmer with its Waterlox tung oil finish," Bryan points out.

One Hundred Acres

A PLACE TO CALL HOME BECOMES A DREAM COME TRUE IN THE RURAL MIDDLE GEORGIA WOODLANDS.

From barn apartment to family farmhouse, the Harris family have embraced their rural setting to live a bucolic lifestyle. After graduating from college, Blake purchased some acreage and then proceeded years later to obtain several additional acres to reach the sum of 100. They cherish the dense woods, the smell of fresh-cut fields, and stargazing at night. After growing up around his grandfather's dairy farm, Blake and wife Kelly planned—along with the late architect Michael Bassett—to realize their dream. They combined a love of beach homes and farmhouses in sketches for planning the project. Treasuring the acreage they own to garden and plant their own food sources, the couple had envisioned their tractor having convenient accommodations on the lower level. Blake is a forester, and he loves nothing more than his John Deere tractor for maintaining the homeplace.

The second floor is designed as the main living area, including the kitchen, dining room, and family room. Rather than separated, the open concept provides a more welcoming space. Much of the cabinetry has been built into the design, with storage and display considerations in the kitchen and family room. Large windows allow plenty of natural light in the fresh, new home structure. Entertaining is quite easy, whether dining or visiting with guests, and there is a casual acceptance that everyone will be included.

The second level tongue-and-groove wooden ceilings were used to emphasize the height, also giving the open feeling the couple desired. Floors were milled in South Georgia with a circular pattern so that wear over the years from foot traffic would not be a concern. A lighter stain

finish was used to contrast with the darker ceiling color. Using samples of various stain tones, a comfortable mid-tone was selected to also wear well with age.

Collected handmade pieces used by great-grandparents and grandparents of the couple were part of the simple life the couple wanted to include on the farm. A favorite room of Kelly's is the nursery, which uses neutrals and tones of green for accent.

Being in their perch at night, the family can now say their forever home wishes came true. The rustic farmhouse setting sets the tone with a sense of warmth and true comfort. Their wish is to preserve and pass down the farm and home to future generations.

Pale gray cabinetry chosen for the kitchen and family room blend well with the reclaimed wood ceilings and natural stone fireplace.

Tonya G. Kilpatrick, the interior designer for the home, used various textiles with plenty of texture. Featuring kelly green striped and monogrammed pillows, the room will transition as their young son grows up with a queen-size bed included. An extra guest bedroom adjoins the nursery with a connecting Jack and Jill bathroom.

A favorite piece is the swing, made by Kelly's grandfather as a housewarming present. It adds to time well spent in the rural Georgia pasture setting.

Higher Ground

PERCHED HIGH IN THE HILLS OF CASHIERS, NORTH CAROLINA, AMID THE QUAINT
SCENIC SETTING OF LONESOME VALLEY, THIS FARMHOUSE-STYLE RETREAT
FILLED WITH MEANINGFUL FAMILY HEIRLOOMS AND TIMEWORN FINISHES
PROVIDES THE PERFECT COUNTRY ESCAPE FOR A FAMILY OF CITY DWELLERS.

The large fireside porch is a favorite family gathering spot with plenty of comfortable wicker furniture and handmade twig tables. Reading, sitting by the fire, visiting with friends, and sipping wine are frequent pastimes enjoyed in this wonderfully airy space.

There is nothing like familiarity when it comes to creating a sense of warmth and comfort. So it seemed the perfect partnership when an Atlanta couple called on interior designer Margaret Bosbyshell to help them plan a cozy mountain retreat and fill it with meaningful family heirlooms that had been passed down for generations. Having worked with these homeowners many times through the years, Margaret considered them not only clients but also good friends.

"This was the fourth home I had worked on for these homeowners, and I also had the pleasure of helping the wife's parents at one time," says the designer, owner of Margaux Interiors Limited based in Atlanta. "As a result, I had lots of insight into their preferences and lifestyle, so I enjoyed the puzzle of figuring out where to use their various pieces of art, rugs, and furniture," she adds.

Designed by Platt Architecture, PA in Brevard, North Carolina, the house—appropriately named "Higher Ground" in honor of the wife's mother's favorite hymn—is nestled amidst scenic Lonesome Valley, an idyllic location in Cashiers, North Carolina, set in the largest box canyon on the East Coast. A residential mountain farm community that celebrates simplicity, family, and nature, the land comprising Lonesome Valley was once a working farm and is laden yet today with a variety of fruit trees, gardens, and charming rustic barns.

When construction began, the homeowners envisioned a comfortable family house nestled beautifully against the mountainside and a color palette that would blend seamlessly into the landscape. As the couple frequently entertains family and friends, they wanted plenty of decks and a

Perfect for gatherings large and small, the cozy dining room features some of the family's cherished heirloom furniture pieces. A vintage antler chandelier and chair seats that are upholstered in a sumptuous patterned fabric create a pleasing contrast against the sleek dark wood antique dining table.

large porch where nature could be enjoyed year-round. Inside, they wanted to be sure to incorporate a collection of Southern antiques from the husband's family in Newnan, Georgia, and the wife's family in Charlotte, North Carolina. When the husband's family passed away, Margaret went to Newnan to look at the furniture to determine what they could use. She absolutely loved it and suggested the pieces to keep for their new mountain home.

"We had so much fun incorporating these special pieces into the design that bring so much character and create happy family memories," Margaret recalls. "The wife's mother also generously invited me to pick out a few pieces of art and furniture from her house for the couple to use in the mountains," she adds.

Cherished heirloom pieces, including a dining room table and chairs, a pair of 1920s twin beds, an antique chest of drawers, a ladder-back chair, and an array of whimsical vintage pottery pieces bring well-worn patina and an unmistakable sense of Old-World appeal to this homey mountain retreat. Intentionally designed to emulate a country farmhouse, the home features classic elements of American farmhouse style that celebrates rustic, relaxed comfort, simplicity, and charm. Constructed with natural wood, rock, copper, reclaimed materials, and lots of hearths for cozy fires, the house also features modern conveniences in the bath, kitchen, garage, and laundry for practicality and to accommodate a contemporary lifestyle. Huge windows and open porches connect the interior spaces to the outdoors, allowing the family to breathe in nature from most any room in the house.

For the interiors, Margaret selected handsome and sumptuous upholsteries that would ultimately provide comfort. Great room fabrics were inspired by the rich, warm hues of an antique Oushak rug as well as an impressive cache of artwork and old pottery. Avid art lovers, the couple has an extraordinary collection of contemporary works from Southern artists mixed with antique prints of landscapes, birds, and animals. A large abstract painting over the great

room mantel creates an impactful focal point, and a collection of Southern pottery lamps and other whimsical pieces layer the room with homey farmhouse charm. The family's antique rocking chair is by far the best seat in the house from which to view the crackling fire.

A remarkable collaboration with the designer, homeowners, architect, builder, landscape designer, and various craftsmen, this project was in every sense a labor of love in a sublime location. From the outset, Margaret ultimately worked to incorporate the family's cherished art, furniture, heirloom pieces, and fresh new furnishings, while also creating comfort and an ease of living that reflects the personality of the homeowners, their color sensibilities, and the culture of the setting.

"When working with any client on a dream home, I first try to understand the family's goals for the house, who will be using it, and how," says Margaret. "This couple was fearless, very open to ideas, and worked diligently to produce a timeless, uniquely beautiful home that they love."

The master bedroom's tongue-and-groove ceiling and subtle color palette creates a relaxing haven for the homeowners. The bed is a family heirloom from the 1920s and is accented with a lovely landscape print hanging above. Patterned draperies bring a pop of color to the whisper-soft hues used throughout this inviting space.

Flanking an antique chest of drawers, a ladderback chair made of applewood is a family heirloom from a 1930s home in Highlands, North Carolina, that belonged to the homeowner's grandparents. The sunflower painting was created by Chattanooga, Tennessee, artist Caroline Sander.

Little Bit Farm

LEAVING THE RUSH OF URBAN LIFE BEHIND, THESE
GEORGIA HOMEOWNERS TRANSFORMED THEIR VACATION
FARMHOUSE INTO A PERMANENT PASTORAL RETREAT.

Living in the city has its undeniable perks, but when the pace of things becomes too hectic, owning a tranquil spot in the country offers a welcome retreat from the hustle and bustle. While they originally called Atlanta their primary address, this Georgia couple found the appeal of their rural property just too enticing to save for sporadic visits. Feeling the tug of a more pastoral life, they made the decision to permanently settle there.

Endearingly called "Little Bit Farm," this bucolic setting of 280 acres just outside of Columbus, Georgia, boasts a refined farmhouse, outdoor amenities, and a large, sustainable garden that provides seasonal, organic produce to a host of area restaurants. "We began renovating the house as a part-time residence in keeping with the couple's weekend stays," says residential designer Robert Norris, co-principal of Atlanta firm Spitzmiller & Norris. "But as they became more and more attached to the land and gardens, the house kept evolving."

Norris and business partner Rick Spitzmiller worked to enlarge the house while staying true to the agrarian nature and context of the place. And since the two architects had worked with these clients on numerous projects in the past, they shared a keen understanding of what best suited the couple and their family. "Appropriately, we chose a vernacular farmhouse aesthetic for the renovation," says Spitzmiller. "The materials used here are all indigenous to the area: stone, pine, cedar, old brick, and large flagstones." Other elements, such as shiplap and board-and-batten siding, as well as slate shingles on the main rooflines and metal standing-seam panels on lower pitches, provide a pleasing roster of textures that are regionally accurate. "The exterior of the house was also painted in a monochromatic color scheme to pull together the stone accents on the additions, chimneys, and porch columns," Spitzmiller says.

Inside, the interplay of brick walls with wood-plank ceilings and reclaimed beams further lends a sense of evolution and time-honored, thoughtful detailing. In the process, the once-meager cottage

The new rocking porch at the entry effectively sets the tone for the entire house. Stone columns adorned with Confederate jasmine further convey a welcoming touch. To maintain the farm's rustic charm, Spitzmiller and Norris consulted with the homeowners on the various structures that dot Little Bit Farm, such as this small chicken coop.

grew to encompass a new front porch and entry hall, a spacious dining room and expanded kitchen, a new wing containing a guest bedroom and master suite, and a gracious screened porch that functions much like an interior room. There's even a recreation/game room for family and friends to enjoy their time together. "The homeowners' overall décor is both casual and refined, which perfectly reflects their lifestyles," says interior designer Lauren DeLoach, who worked with the clients on selecting fabrics and culling through furniture pieces from their previous home. "Likewise, their large collection of books and earthen jugs brought an extra layer of personality to the farmhouse."

Rounding out the design team, landscape architect Richard Anderson enabled the couple to see their property with a fresh pair of eyes, particularly in the placement and spacing of key outdoor features. "I sought to create a connection between elements that agreed with the lay of the land instead of clustering them all together in one area," says Anderson. Those elements include terraced lawns, a subtly placed swimming pool, bocce and badminton courts, a hedged fountain garden, and a cleverly located parking barn. The landscape architect also rerouted the main drive to create a more flattering approach to the farmhouse.

When it came to introducing additional landscaping, Anderson didn't just stick to indigenous plants but instead chose a variety that have earned a successful track record for the region. "I wasn't interested in an 'ornamental' landscape. I wanted one that both created spaces and led you through them," he explains. Trees such as Japanese snowballs, eastern cedars, and crepe myrtles, coupled with well-placed boxwoods, hollies, and azaleas, help to shade and enhance the property without overpowering it. "Even rural farms often have hedges and boxwoods planted around the main house as finishing touches, but as you venture into the surrounding property, things become more natural and relaxed," Anderson says. "Come to think of it, that observation perfectly describes the dual nature of this well-coordinated project."

This new wing was added during the renovation, which includes this spacious master bedroom suite. Highlighted with large windows and an entire wall framed with bookcases, the tranquil space allows the homeowners to get away from the daily responsibilities of running a farm.

The downstairs bunk room emits a camp-like quality that's perfect for younger members of the family.

RESOURCES

Editor: Cindy Smith Cooper
Senior Art Director: Tracy Wood Franklin
Senior Copy Editor: Rhonda Lee Lother

Cover: Photography by Mark Lohman, styling by Sunday Hendrickson.

Introduction, 8–11: Text by Jeanne Delathouder.

Colonial Charm, 12–21: Photography by Rob Karosis; text by Bethany Adams; architect: Jimmy Crisp, Crisp Architects, 845-677-8256; crisparchitects.com; builder: George Carrothers, georgecarrothers@hotmail.com.

Refined Rustic, 22–35: Photography by Heidi Long; text by Bethany Adams; architect: Janet Jarvis, The Jarvis Group, Architects, AIA, PLLC, www.jarvis-group.com.

A Personal Touch, 36–45: Photography by Alise O'Brien; text by Bethany Adams; interior design by Amy Studebaker and Michelle Thore, Amy Studebaker Design, 314-440-0853, amystudebakerdesign.com; architect: David Pape, Pape Studio, Inc., 314-781-4008.

Cultivating Home, 46–53: Photography by John O'Hagan; text by Elizabeth Czapski.

New Victorian Era, 54–65: Photography by Kate Sears; text by K. Faith Morgan.

Cloverfield Farm, 66–75: Photography by Lincoln Barbour; text by Bethany Adams; builder: Jonathan Burch; architects: Doug Enoch, 901-685-7636, dougenoch.com, and David Anderson, 901-786-8494, davidandersonarchitect.com.

Close to Home, 76–89: Photography by Lauren Rubenstein; text by Hannah Jones; contractor: John Bynum, John Bynum Custom Homes, 678-725-2848, bynumhomes.com.

Cottage to Farmhouse, 90–101: Photography by Jim Bathie; text by Cindy Smith Cooper; interior design by Sunni Glidewell and Pandy Agnew; architect: Jordan Hostetler, David Acton Building Corporation, davidactonbuilding.com.

Californian Charm, 102–111: Photography by Mark Lohman; text by Bethany Adams; styling by Sunday Hendrickson.

Storied Style on the Lake, 112–125: Photography by Lincoln Barbour; text by Bethany Adams; architect: Keith Summerour, Summerour Architects, 404-603-8585, summerour.net; interior design by The Design Atelier, 404-365-8662, thedesignatelier.com; contractor: Marbury McCullough, TCC General Contractors, 256-392-4115, tcccontractors.com.

The Honeymoon Home, 126–137: Photography by Tria Giovan; text by Hannah Jones; location: J&D Farms, janddfarms.com.

Modern Country Style, 138–147: Photography by Robin Stubbert/Gap Interiors; text by Gap Interiors; architect: Wayne Swodron; styling by Susan Burns.

The Beauty of the Earth, 148–161: Photography by Alison Gootee, Holland Williams; text by Bethany Adams; interior design by Ashley Gilbreath, 334-262-3231, ashleygilbreath.com; architect: Andy Smith, Andy Smith Architecture, 334-318-4332; builder: Joseph Darley, Darley Construction, 334-983-9177.

The Good Life, 162–169: Photography by Robin Stubbert; text by Jeanne Delathouder.

A Passion for Preservation, 170–181: Photography by Jim Bathie; text by Bethany Adams; architect: Eliot Goss, 307-413-6837, eliotgossarchitect.com; builder: Joe Montesano, Wilkinson-Montesano, 307-733-9581, wilkinson-montesano.com.

Paradise Rebuilt, 182–189: Photography by John O'Hagan; text by Robert C. Martin; architect: Al Platt; interior design by Maxine and Jeff Sikes.

One Hundred Acres, 190–199: Photography by James Wilson; text by Cindy Smith Cooper; interior design by Tonya G. Kilpatrick; architect: Michael Bassett.

Higher Ground, 200–207: Photography by Mac Jamieson; text by Jeanne Delathouder; interior design by Margaret Bosbyshell, Margaux Interiors Limited, 404-276-1997, info@margauxinteriorslimited.com; architect: Platt Architecture, PA.

Little Bit Farm, 208–217: Photography by Marcy Black Simpson; text by Robert C. Martin; architect: Frederick Spitzmiller and Robert Norris of Spitzmiller and Norris, Inc.; interior design by Lauren DeLoach of Lauren DeLoach Interiors; landscape design by Rick Anderson; construction by Johnny Cargill.